THE
BODY
MUTINIES

THE
BODY
MUTINIES

Lucia Perillo

PURDUE UNIVERSITY PRESS / WEST LAFAYETTE, INDIANA

The paper used in this book meets the minimum requirements of
American National Standard for Information Sciences—Permanence of
Paper for Printed Library Materials, ANSI Z39.48-1992. ⊛

Printed in the United States of America
Design by Chiquita Babb

Library of Congress Cataloging-in-Publication Data
Perillo, Lucia Maria, 1958–
    The body mutinies / Lucia Perillo
      p.   cm.
    ISBN 1-55753-083-1 (pbk.)
    I. Title.
    PS 3566.E69146B63 1996
    811'.54—dc20   95-45711
                                          CIP

ACKNOWLEDGMENTS

These poems first appeared, in earlier drafts, in the following publications: *The American Voice, The Atlantic, The Black Warrior Review, The Chronicle for Higher Education, The Journal, The Kenyon Review, Left Bank, The Mississippi Valley Review, Northwest Review, Ontario Review, Ploughshares, Poet Lore, Poetry East, Quarterly West, Seattle Review, Syracuse Scholar, The Third Coast, Willow Springs, ZYZZYVA.*

"Skin" appeared in *The Best American Poems 1993.* "The Roots of Pessimism in Model Rocketry, the Fallacy of Its Premise" appeared in *What Will Suffice: Contemporary American Poets on the Art of Poetry.*

This work was made possible in part from funds granted to the author by the Charles H. Revson Foundation, and I would like to extend my thanks to PEN / Revson judges Honor Moore, Robert Peters, and Robert Phillips, as well as to Tess Gallagher for encouraging my application for this award in the first place. I am also indebted to Saint Martin's College, Southern Illinois University, and my family for financial support that enabled the writing of these poems.

It would be very cumbersome to acknowledge here the many people whose rigorous criticism and enthusiastic support have shaped these poems; I am hoping they know who they are. And know how grateful I am for the careful readings that I did not always graciously receive.

For Jim, my own private Yaddo

—But people are like wolves to me!

*—You mustn't say that, Kaspar.
Look at Florian—he lost his father
in an accident, he is blind, but
does he complain? No, he plays the
piano the whole day and it doesn't
matter that his music sounds a little
strange.*

—Werner Herzog
The Enigma of Kaspar Hauser

CONTENTS

I

II

III

IV

I

*Why be given a body if you have to keep it
shut up in a case like a rare, rare fiddle?*

—Katherine Mansfield

HOW WESTERN UNDERWEAR
CAME TO JAPAN

When Tokyo's Shirokiya Drygoods caught fire
in the thirties, shopgirls tore the shelves' kimonos
and knotted them in ropes. Older women used
both hands, descending safely from the highest floors
though their underskirts flew up around their hips.

The crowded street saw everything beneath—
ankles, knees, the purple flanges of their sex.
Versus the younger girls' careful keeping
one hand pinned against their skirts, against
the nothing under them and their silk falling.

SKIN

Back then it seemed that wherever a girl took off her clothes
        the police would find her—
in the backs of cars or beside the dark night ponds, opening
        like a green leaf across
some boy's knees, the skin so white and taut beneath the moon
        it was almost too terrible,
too beautiful to look at, a tinderbox, though she did not know.
        But the men who came
beating the night rushes with their flashlights and thighs—
        they knew. About Helen,
about how a body could cause the fall of Troy and the death
        of a perfectly good king.
So they read the boy his rights and shoved him spread-legged
        against the car
while the girl hopped barefoot on the asphalt, cloaked
        in a wool rescue blanket.
Or sometimes girls fled so their fathers wouldn't hit them,
        their white legs flashing as they ran.
And the boys were handcuffed just until their wrists had welts
        and let off half a block from home.

God, for how many years did I believe there were truly laws
        against such things,
laws of adulthood: no yelling out of cars in traffic tunnels,
        no walking without shoes,
no singing any foolish songs in public places. Or else
        they could lock you in jail
or, as good as condemning you to death, tell both your lower-
        and upper-case Catholic fathers.
And out of all these crimes, unveiling the body was of course
        the worst, as though something

4

about the skin's phosphorescence, its surface as velvet as
    a deer's new horn,
could drive not only men but civilization mad, could lead us
    to unspeakable cruelties.
There were elders who from experience understood these things
    much better than we.
And it's true, remembering I had that kind of skin does drive me
    half-crazy with loss.
Skin that to me now so much resembles a broad white lily
    on the first morning it unfurls.

INSEMINATOR MAN

When I call him back now, he comes dressed in the silver of
    memory,
silver coveralls and silver boots
and a silver hard hat that makes no sense.
The cows could not bombard his head,
though the Lilies and Buttercups, the Jezebels and Mathildas,
avenged their lot in other ways
like kicking over a pail or stomping his foot.
Blue welt, the small bones come unknitted,
the big toenail a black cicada peeling off its branch.

         * *

It wasn't hard to understand their grudge, their harbor
    of accumulated hurts—
imagine lugging those big tits everywhere, year after year.
Balloons full of wet concrete
hung between their legs like scrotums, duplicate and puffed.
I remember grappling with the nipples
like a teenage boy in a car's back seat
and how the teats would always fill again before I could complete
    their squeezing-out.
At night, two floors above them in the half-demolished barn,
my hands ached and made me dream of cows that drained
until the little stool rose off the ground and I found myself
    dog-paddling in milk.

         * *

The summer after college I'd gone off to live with women
who'd forsworn straight jobs and underwear and men.
At night the ten of us linked hands
around a low wirespool table before we took our meals of

vegetables and bread.
Afterward, from where the barn's missing wall
opened out on Mad River, which had no banks but cut an oxbow
flush with the iridescent green swale of the lower fields,
I saw women bathing, their white flanks in dim light
rising like mayflies born straight out of the river.

                              *   *

Everyone else was haying the lower field when he pulled up,
his van unmarked and streamlined like his wares:
vials of silvery jism from a bull named Festus
who—because he'd sired a jersey that took first place
at the Vermont state fair in '53—
was consigned to hurried couplings with an old maple stump
rigged up with white fur and a beaker.
When the man appeared I was mucking stalls in such heat
that I can't imagine whether or not I would have worn
          my shirt
or at what point it became clear to me that the bull Festus
          had been dead for years.

                              *   *

I had this idea the world did not need men:
not that we would have to kill them personally
but through our sustained negligence they would soon die off
like houseplants. When I pictured the afterlife
it was like an illustration in one of those Jehovah's Witness
          magazines,
all of us, cows and women, marching on a promised land
colored that luminous green and disencumbered by breasts.
I slept in the barn on a pallet of fir limbs,

ate things I dug out of the woods,
planned to make love only with women, then changed my mind
when I realized how much they scared me.

* *

"Inseminator man," he announced himself, extending a hand,
though I can't remember we actually spoke.
We needed him to make the cows dry off and come into new milk:
we'd sell the boy-calves for veal, keep the females for milkers,
and Festus would live on, with this man for a handmaid,
whom I met as he was either going into the barn or coming out.
I know for a fact he didn't trumpet his presence,
        but came and went mysteriously
like the dove that bore the sperm of God to earth.

* *

He wore a hard hat, introduced himself before I took him in,
and I remember how he graciously ignored my breasts while still
        giving them wide berth.
Maybe I wore a shirt or maybe not: to say anything
        about those days now sounds so strange.
We would kill off the boys, save the females for milkers
        I figured,
as I led him to the halfway mucked-out stalls, where he
        unfurled a glove past his elbow
like Ava Gardner in an old-movie nightclub scene.
Then greased the glove with something from a rusted can
        before I left him in the privacy of barn light
with the rows of cows and the work of their next generation
while I went back outside to the shimmering and nearly
        blinding work of mine.

8

DURABLE GOODS

The cast-iron tub has stood on its claw feet
as long as the house has been here, eighty years,
and now a trough is worn into its surface,
an ellipsoid shaped like a child with swaddled limbs.
Rump thighs calves . . . the twin globes of footheels . . .
all those buttery gobbets of dark meat marked
where they made off with the porcelain.
Where body settled into the space of body,
a more or less of more alike than not . . .

So while the woman soaps her breasts
and rehearses Piaf, or the man turns the newspaper
back to pulp where he touches with his wet thumbs,
civilizations change hands, mountains
break open, rivers will wash away their banks.
Perspiration gathers in fine hair above her lip
until finally she lets herself go under.
The water swallows with a glubbing sound.
And he rises from the tub and towels dry,
puts on clothes to greet the day, believing
a puddle on the floor is all he leaves behind.

THE LIFE OPAQUE

As the television flickers, the docudrama unravels,
the blue half-moons half-swallow our eyes.
These are the women he chooses: so young
they wear none of the creases of history,
yet old enough their skin leaks musk and salts
so he can track their scent for miles.
Hollywood has even made the killer
lovely, less than a human presence—
his onslaughts lacking any trace,
like snow blanketing a field, the screen
going dark to bless him with uncertain grace
at precisely that moment the skulls would break
under the arc of his crowbar, or his log or pipe
. . . going dark, like the sky above the Cascades
when he shovels mountain soil into their eyes.

When the lights come up again, they're full of words
from our sponsors—tampon, deodorant, powder.
For one bright minute, each box or cylinder
is held toward us in an upturned palm. They
have names like *Safe* and *Secure* and *Free*—
these gifts that are supposed to render us
transparent, able to stalk our lives
without scarring a branch, without scenting
any leaf. Like the magic ghostshirts
worn by the Sioux, who believed their mortal bodies
now had been hidden from the cavalry—
but of course the flesh proved stubborn.
The bullets went in their chests and came out their backs
and their ponies rode on, riderless.

LOST INNOCENCE OF THE POTATO GIVERS

They're just a passing phase. All are symptoms
of our times and the confusion around us.
  —Reverend Billy Graham on The Beatles

At first we culled our winnings from the offering
    of fists—
one potato, two potato—until we realized that such
    random calibration
was no real test of love. So we cultivated pain:
    hunkering on the macadam
sun-baked for hours in the schoolyard, our panties
    bunched beneath our skirts.
The girl who could sit there longest would gain title
    to the most handsome Beatle, Paul.
John George Ringo—the rest were divvied according to
    whose buttocks were most scarlet.
And when our fourth-grade teacher asked why we wore such
    tortured looks through long division,
we shrugged, scritching our pencils over fleshy shapes
    of hearts and flowers.

Ed Sullivan started it, his chiseled and skeletal stub
    of a head, his big shoe
stomping our loyalties to the man-boys Dion
    and Presley.
Even priggish neighbor Emily said I had to kneel before
    the TV as though praying.
Then the pixels assembled the audience's exploding
    like a carcass when it's knifed,
and I copied the pose assumed on-screen: hands pressed
    against sides of my skull
like the bald dwarf who stands goggle-eyed on a jetty
    in Munch's painting, and screams.

My mother rushed to the basement, a dishrag dripping
   from her soaped hand.
What's wrong? she yelled. *Are you hurt? What in godsname
   is all this screaming?*

February 1964: Johnson's choppers were whopping up the sky
   over the Gulf of Tonkin.
Despite the tacit code of silence about the war, somehow
   they must have known:
on television, girls were brawling drunkenly and raking
   fingernails across their cheeks,
ripping their own hair in vicious chunks, as though beauty
   were suddenly indulgent or profane.
That night in Saigon's Capital Kinh-Do Theatre, three GIs
   got blown up during a strip show.
But of course I didn't know that. I couldn't have even
   found Saigon on a map.
Girls were going limp in the arms of riot-geared policemen,
   who carried them off like the dead,
and my mother was stunned when she saw I'd torn my shirt
   over my not-yet-breasts.

After that, I kept everything a secret, the self-inflicted
   burns and scars and nicks.
I was doing it for love love love: the stones in my shoes,
   the burrs in my shirt,
the mother-of-pearl penknife I used for cutting grooves
   in my thumb or palm
whenever I needed to swear some blood pact with another
   disenthralled potato giver.
We spent recess practicing how to stick our tongues

in Paul's imaginary mouth,
letting everything drain out until we were limp, nothing,
    sucked right into the earth.
Then we would mash our bodies against the schoolyard's wide
    and gray-barked beech,
which was cruel and strong and unrelenting, smooth and cold,
    the way we hoped our husbands would be.

THE PROFESSOR WONDERS IF HIS
DAUGHTER WILL UNDERSTAND TRAGEDY

Indignation is the soul's defense against
the wound of doubt.

—Allan Bloom

Two bottles of wine to reach this conclusion:
now that he's sixty, one thing he regrets
is never buying an M16 while they were legal
and going into the record department at Woolworth's
or K-Mart or maybe even a whole store devoted to
those jungle rhythms. He imagines firing
a couple of rounds into the stacked LPs,
sending black shards everywhere. His daughter,
he says, he can't count the nights he heard her
screeching along with those idiot refrains.
That must be why her life is such a shambles:
it was like an exorcism going on up there.
And tonight he realizes that if he'd had the courage,
he might have saved her. Bellini, Verdi, Bizet . . .
they'd probably fall too by the wayside,
a submachine gun unable to spare his beloveds
and at the same time avenge them. And suddenly
that makes him sad, to think
of the gypsy girl lying dead in the shop aisles,
the final chorus of "Love is a rebellious bird . . ."
welling up like blood while Don José cries:
Arrest me . . . I killed her . . . Carmen! My adored Carmen!

TRIPE

We were never a family given to tongue or brains.
So the cow's stomach had to bear her last straws,
had to be my mother's warning-bell that chops and roasts
and the parched breasts of chickens, the ribs and legs
and steaks and fish and even the calf's sour liver
had become testaments to the monotony of days.
Since then I have understood the rebellion hedged
in its bifurcated rind, its pallor, its refusal
to tear or shred when chawed on by first
the right then the left jaw's teeth—
until finally the wad must be swallowed whole.

The tough meat meant life's repertoire had shrunk
to a sack inside of which she was boxing shadows—
kids and laundry, yes, but every night the damned
insistence of dinner. And wasn't the stomach
a master alchemist: grass and slops and the green dirt
transformed into other cuts of bloody, marbled beef.
Times when she wanted that same transformation
the house filled with its stewing, a ghastly sweet
that drove us underneath the beds. From there
we braved mushroom clouds rising off her electric range,
blowing the kitchen walls as wide as both Dakotas.
And I pictured her pale-faced & lustrous with steam
as she stood out in that new open space, lifting
the hair off her neck as the stock pot billowed
its sugary haze like the sweat of a hired man.

ON THE SUNKEN FISH PROCESSOR
TENYO MARU

Just as we pray that the *Tenyo Maru* keeps its hull intact
    as it yaws and rocks
on the ocean floor off Cape Flattery, a quarter million barrels
    of crude oil inside—
so too are we warned against breaching the social contract,
    that glass eye rolling
in our human creek. For what might happen if we lift
    the codicils on belching?
If sex were permitted in the shopping malls? If people
    were allowed to sing arias
from *Don Giovanni,* loudly and out of tune, waiting in line
    at Department of Motor Vehicles?
And I remember Dr. Daniel Thompson at the Denver Wildlife
    Research Center,
whose hair was pale as a baby's, who, after telling me about
    his being born again
and consequent belief in all men being created in the image
    of Christ,
said that I'd better get some new clothes or I'd be fired.
    And furthermore—poor eggshell
heart, poor lungs made of toast—That I smelled funny.
    At first I didn't believe him.
But right away I realized that my shirt was stained
    and needed tucking in,
and when I took it off that night I found a greasy half-
    moon under each sleeve.
So at the Goodwill store I bought some clothes that had
    no doubt belonged to dead Republicans,
ladies who shipped their sons to war, a King James
    in their armpits as they waved.

Since then I have kept a check on what emissions
        steal out of my body,
and I feel the gray alluvium of pity silting up my throat
        whenever hard luck's ambassadors
crash the gate I've erected via this scrubbed husk.
        Which I distinctly remember twice:
once in Chicago, a black woman whose hair stood in the high
        crocheted hat of poverty,
her body resembling a huge plastic doll, the Saucy Walker
        I was given as a child and soon defaced,
her legs bare from the thighs to purple sneakers, even though
        the December cold was breaking records.
She was not afraid to sing in the subway, and I wondered if
        she welcomed those spaces
her song could fill as we riders moved into adjacent cars,
        so redolent was her music.
But she was the kind of woman you'd expect to smell
        poor and crazy,
and I am more at a loss to explain the other, the woman
        who resembled Simone Weil,
her dark hair pulled in a pilgrim bun, her brow furrowed,
        her stick limbs clothed
in a nurse's tunic and yellowed slacks, marching up
        and down the empty library aisles
where she had laid placards she was filling with capital
        blue letters from Leviticus.
I'm not talking now about the merely odorous, but rankness
        an order of magnitude removed
from the gamy hobos who live beneath the railroad trestle
        and make their living collecting cans.

A stink from the parishes of women, the frank incense
        of all our druid witchery,
the gristle that stuck in Daniel Thompson's craw when he
        began to hem and haw and cough up
the word *hygiene* like a dirty hankie. For how many years
        has he made me so ashamed?
August now, sweating like something twirled around a spit,
        I'm thinking of those tons of fish
dead in their hold beneath the ocean, a secret depth charge,
        the sea scrubbing them
and scrubbing, like me so hungry for December and the safety
        of my thick black coat.

AT SAINT PLACID'S

She wears a habit the unlikely blue color
of a swimming pool, the skin of her face
smooth where it shows beneath a wimple
from which one blond strand escapes.
While she squints at the sun, her hands
knit themselves in the folds of her skirts.
The man she's speaking to, the monk,
is also young, his shoulders broad
from shooting baskets in the gym.
I have seen him running across the fields
in his nylon shorts, big muscles like roasts
sheathing the bones in his thighs.
They are standing on the monastery's walkway
and I am at the window watching
this moment when their voices fall away,
nothing left but the sound of water dripping
off the trees, a fuchsia brooding in a basket
over her left shoulder. Silent now,
they are thinking. But not
about that. The fine weather, yes,
the church bells, the cross, an old woman
who used to come to mass who's dying.
All this they think of. But surely
not about that, no. Not that other thing.

CHEKHOV'S CRUELTY,
CHEKHOV'S GRACE

1.

All the talk these days is Chekhov.
And all the writers have made their homage known:
how they gave up drinking because of Chekhov,
how they saved their marriages because of Chekhov,
how they pulled the gun barrels from their mouths
in the nick of time when some line of Chekhov's
galloped suddenly into their heads . . . though in the end
his graces are left stubbornly unexplained.
Maybe it's the way the story hangs
on the smallest of details, the narrator
lingering like a camera on the woman's hand
as it moves to touch the brooch stuck on her throat.

2.

Today two actors from New York are doing scenes
from *The Seagull,* using a rolled towel
for the dead bird that cinches their unravelling.
I lay this sea gull at your feet, he says.
She says, *Forgive me, but I don't understand it.*
The actors tell us how they prowled for days
the city waterfront, with a .22 for shooting
a blue-gray hinge out of the sky: opening night
had a plume of blood tethered to its beak.
And they must have become lovers, even my students
can see how tenderly his fingers brush her cheek
in this monastery classroom, its ceiling

fallen to show us the pale laths underneath.
Outside, monks are marching across the courtyard
like darker birds, their robes flapping
against bony heels that remind us: how everyone
will get exactly what they want and then despise it—
Konstantine will kill himself, Nina will go mad
and the beauty is how none of this will stop them.
Act one: look how willingly the actors seal their lips
in a kiss that seems, at least for now, without an end.

DEATH GETS A CHAIR

This damn ranting about doom . . .
is that food for modern minds?
                    —from Ingmar Bergman's *The Seventh Seal*

The Swedes look good in black and white
because they're so fair, so blond.
On film, the knight Antonius's skin
shines as though there's a lamp inside his body.
Even when they've come down with the plague,
their reaper is robust, the kind of guy
who'd work the dancing bears at carnivals
were it not for his scythe and hood.
But because the characters—three acrobats,
the blacksmith and his wife, the squire—
command such good blood and sturdy bones,
we assume they'll escape his grip somehow,
or reveal themselves as privy to a joke
whose punch line is withheld until the end.
This story—Knight and Death play chess—
has always been the butt of parody:
Death plays checkers, Death plays tennis,
Death plays badminton in the short film
that cracks me up—where American actors
pretend they're speaking Swedish.
You call your own spoof *Death Gets a Chair:*
Death has to wander around Chicago
looking for a chair before the game begins.
Your Death has got the mannerisms down:
thrusting out his right arm like a signpost,
cloak outstretched, his tithe demanded *Now!*—
this some galoot from your film class
wearing hightop sneakers, a UNLV sweatshirt
showing under his robe each time he tries

to make that insistent motion with his hand.
Death tries to wrestle a patio chair
from a woman in curlers whose beefcake husband
finally knocks him off the fire escape.
All of Bergman's weighty questions answered
(*Why can't I kill the God who lives inside me?*
Why must he live on in this humiliating way?)
with a store mannequin, a little ketchup
doused on its robe after splatting in the alley.
But Bergman knew Death doesn't need a chair—
he sits on beach stones, on tree roots,
he plays chess kneeling on the hard planks
in the church confessional. And wins.
I guess the message is: Keep up your guard.
So when you tell me your newest lover
is a man, I say *Be careful* not *Be happy.*
I see the specter hunched over his board,
advancing his rook, I hear the fresco painter
in the church nave telling the knight:
You should see the boils in a diseased man's throat.
Last month I heard the young writer speak
about his life as a man who loves men
and is dying. Kaposi's had already moved
into his lungs, so his breathing was labored
and weak, his voice full of sand.
He started out saying he'd just been put
on the waiting list to place his ashes
in the columbarium at Saint John the Divine,
but nobody knew how to laugh at a joke like that.
In *The Seventh Seal,* the twist comes learning
that all along there was no joke, no secret;

Death had always laid his few cards on the table.
What I don't understand is how a lamb, with its hoof,
could have broken the seals that bound
the Book of Revelation, which supposedly
loosed the fire and turned the sea to blood.
How could a lamb do any damn such thing?
And why would God make himself incarnate
in an animal so likely to be slaughtered?
I mean, why wouldn't God have chosen a crow
or a jackal, some beast the Nazarenes
would never think to eat? I mean
if your choice is your life in one hand
versus *your life* in the other, how do you choose?
I'm not being a priss, I just want to know.

II

"She would of been a good woman," The Misfit said, "if it had been somebody there to shoot her every minute of her life."

—Flannery O'Connor,
"A Good Man Is Hard to Find"

ON A STREETCORNER IN MERIDA

The color of the woman's face kept changing
as she walked in and out of slatted light
cast on the sidewalk by gaps between white buildings.
In her arms a burlap sack that squalled so hard
she had to keep it pinned between her elbow and her hip
and wrestle with it every time she crossed a block.

At the bus stop finally she let it spill:
a copper-colored pig, made still by the sudden light,
blinking and backing in the corner of two stucco walls.
When the woman saw us watching from across the street,
a muffled laughter ran from her like water.
Her eyes were very white; her face was red—

we were laughing too but, come to think of it, her face
was red: as though we'd caught her in an act of shame
or weakness. She looked down at her boy
who was kneeling on the pavement, his arm
extended with a sugar plug held to the shying pig.
When sweetness lured the animal, you touched my hip.

But wasn't there a heaviness
like yours in his outstretched limb, as he coaxed
the pig to bend its neck into the sack, its quarter
of the common, unrelenting future? As if the boy knew
his job will be to catch the entrails in a plastic bowl
when his mother carves the animal from groin to throat.

There is no sentiment inside an empty belly,
but still I want to know if just before its butchering

the pig felt deceived by the firm embrace
with which she must have held it on the bus ride out of town.
If the boy wept, or simply looked off at the sundown,
or in his small hand quietly took up her bloody palm.

THE ROOTS OF PESSIMISM IN MODEL
ROCKETRY, THE FALLACY OF ITS PREMISE

X-Ray had a see-thru payload chamber.
The Flying Saucer model was a gyp—
unless you were the kind of kid who loved
the balsa wood shredding more than flight time,
the smashing down more than the going up.
When Big Bertha sheared my brother's pinkie
I watched medicine make its promise good:
in the future we would all be androids.
The doctors reinstalled his milky nail
and drained blue fingertip, though afterward
I felt a little cheated. Already
I'd envisioned how his mutant terrors
could be put to my use, the naked stub .
unsheathed to jinx an enemy sneaker.

We were a tribe of Josef Mengeles
doing frontier science: putting crickets
in the payload, betting if they'd return
alive or dead. I always bet on death
because they always came down dead, I was
the pessimist, the child of many coins.
When someone fished from the dusty ballfield
the cocktail sausage of my brother's loss,
I gave its odds less than even money.
My vote was: Put the finger in a can,
send it to Estes Model Rocket Co.
who would feel guilty enough to send cash.
But guilt turned on me. Now my brother's hand
looks perfect, except when he makes a fist.

THE BODY MUTINIES

—outside Saint Pete's

When the doctor runs out of words and still
I won't leave, he latches my shoulder and
steers me out doors. Where I see his blurred hand,
through the milk glass, flapping goodbye like a sail
(& me not griefstruck yet but still amazed: how
words and names—medicine's blunt instruments—
undid me. And the seconds, the half seconds
it took for him to say those words.) For now,
I'll just stand in the courtyard, watching bodies
struggle in then out of one lean shadow
a tall fir lays across the wet flagstones,
before the sun clears the valance of gray trees
and finds the surgical-supply shop window
and makes the dusty bedpans glint like coins.

RETABLO WITH MULTIPLE SCLEROSIS
AND SAINTS

Every angel is terrifying.
> —Rainer Maria Rilke, *Duino Elegies*

Rilke was a jerk.
> —John Berryman, *The Dreamsongs*

For Vivian Kendall

Saint Joseph for the good death.
Camillus for protection against sickness of the feet.
And Saint Liberata, whose miraculous beard
sprouted to save her from being married to a king—
for when marriage delivers the wrong god in its machine,

however splendid he appears. Then soon your husband
stops taking his meds, and then he's coming down
with visions: your pores smoking like a fleet
of ancient Cadillacs. Late nights find him studying you
—wrench in his one hand and knife in the other—

torn between demolition and repair. Saint Veronica,
patron of hemorrhage, Raphael the Archangel of escape . . .
I'm guessing now about by what miracle's grace
you flew from that coop to this coop of a room
where I'm watching your brush work the latest version

of your face: this one jowled like a yam and floating
where a black cloud threatens to digest your legs.
And it's making me shaky, as if we've boarded a train
whose engineer passed caution three fingers of whiskey ago.
From here, we're riding the caboose full of stumblers.

Each night I try to memorize the fit of my own legs
in case my waking finds them shadowy and numb;
I don't want any limb to think I am ungrateful
for swimming lengths of the ice-blue pool.
Or for the soup spoon's lifting, or for the swallowing . . .

I remember the Strait of Juan de Fuca's thundering
(San Juan: patron of baptism, patron of water)
when my bladder opened like a floodgate.
No one was there to watch me rinse in the sea, but still
that moment glimmered with how wildly someday we might float:

jellyfish, medusas, for whom the lighthouse
is just a shadow darkening the voyage on bright days.
But the clouds were flat and blatant—
like clouds in religious iconography, pedestals
for the retablo's apparition, swooping down

to save us. And with a wet hem slapping at
my knees, I thought of Frida Kahlo, whose long skirt
hid a withered leg and one foot crushed
when the bus she was riding got hit by a train
and a piece of it came out, good christ, between her legs.

In her self-portraits, I always see
the mirror turned back on this event: Frida shedding tears
or bandaged, Frida bartering her form's grotesqueries,
Frida never letting the body's trauma match
the dispassion worn so stiffly in her face—like a dog

wearing one of those broad, clownlike ruffs
so it can't gnaw or even see what's going on below.
Like the game she loved: Cadavre Exquis.
On folded paper, each player sketches one part
of a figure, so when the whole is finally displayed

the joke lies in discovering the body's sum.
Kahlo always drew genitals—big and pronged
and dripping cum or loopy: she knew
we're always being sucked into that center
around which all this other business spins—

Painting, Poetry, Marx, God.
The unfolded life is uglier than we planned
but the genitals *are* exquisite, they are such
strange flowers, carnivorous & tropical.
And they will die if they can't eat.

Today I read that Kahlo's art has become
the rage, inflated, one of her self-portraits auctioned off
for more than a million bucks. The critic
called those two hundred replications of her face
a self-indulgence—doesn't everybody live with some degree

of pain? *Well, true enough,* I'm thinking as I watch
your brush steer your own flying head through space,
but christ, Viv: by the end she only had one fucking leg!—
how was she supposed to paint the world if she couldn't
even stagger round the block? And I am sick

of the way the miracles have all been relegated
to those TV shows that come on after ten o'clock at night,
when the soul ascends into its reenacted crib of light
above the operating table, while the camera jiggles
until far-flung America comes dialing in. How cute the angels

have become out there, how quaint the Virgin's intercession.
Meanwhile the saints stand nicknamed in the halls
of hospitals where the doctors are such screw-ups
even death gets botched. But here in your workroom
let's throw in Saint Rita: our lady of the last ditch,

impossibility's patron. Whose name can't help
conjuring a waitress in the only diner left in town
and the waterfalling of a bellied pot, the coffee
caught forever in one-half a perfect lancet arch
in our sloppy and hungover visions of being saved.

What we need, my friend,
is that Rita kind of salvation, a miracle
trapped by the crudest grace.
No need for shapeliness or color.
No need for lines converging at a point in space—

just the saint
and the body
and the story that ends with the body raised.
And a few words to tell the story of the story
scrawled at the bottom of this (albeit crude) tin plate.

FLESH TOOTH HOUSE

I dreamed I lived inside a tiny house
whose softwood floor was rotting underneath
my feet. Outside were muddy fields of stubble corn
and the sea was not far off.

When the horses came, they came
in the usual way that horses enter dreaming.
A shadow crossed my northern window: her dark mane
arced and fell, indistinct and blurring.

When I swung the door to greet her,
she was waiting on the porch. But only bones
were holding up the speckled hide, her swollen joints
like galls along a branch.

And I am ashamed to say how fast
I shut the door on bearing witness. How relieved
to hear the porch's clop and creak as she passed off.
And now—how hard this keeping up

a trust in flesh, tooth, house,
when the metaphors we count on being solid
shift their ground. Through a window I watched her
trail away behind another starving horse—

their gait was wobbling and unsteady.
Yet sure in their deliverance to a far cluster
of pines. As though, though they were close to death,
they were at the same time very far away.

ELEPHANT

The story was about the man who bore his family
—an aging mother, an unemployed brother, a son—
on his back like an elephant. And though the author
was not slow in its telling, he sometimes paused
to draw air to what lungs the surgeon
had left him, his breathing made loud by the P.A.
For many minutes, words fell from him
like drumming rain, insisting his presence,
insisting what the body can continue on in spite of.
Afterwards, signing the paperback I bought,
he put it into smaller words: *Take care of yourself.*

Walking to my car, I thought about how he was led
from the store by a woman with jewels in her hair
who looked after his steps. And I thought
of my mother, how she brings the ampule
and the teacup to my father's bed. How even
this dark sidewalk must have someone to sweep it clean.
But then a bulky creature with broad gray sides
appeared before me, wedged into a storefront.
A man in a wheelchair was settling for night, crutches
braced in an X barricading harm beyond the doorframe,
his watch cap pulled to dull his ears and eyes.

I told myself he was okay: when he's hungry,
why, he just hums a little tune that halts the gnawing.
And when there's any place his chair can't take him
he's always got a bottle that'll bring him there.
And when it's raining, even when it's pissing like a horse
he's some place dry. After all, this is America,

where we are raised on stories of the little trains
and creatures who endure because their hearts are pure,
their nerves are steel. Only the weak among us
think they need someone beyond themselves, and falter.
Not this man. Look at him: he'll find ways of taking care.

KILNED

I was trying somehow to keep my works
true to their nature, to allow the crudeness
to be their beauty.

—Stephen Lang

These days when blood refuses to be talked into the stone,
when the legs twitch like hounds under the sheets
and the eyes are troubled by a drifting fleck—
I think of him: the artist
who climbs into the lava runs at Kalapana,
the only person who has not fled from town
fearing the advance of basalt tongues.
He wears no special boots, no special clothes,
no special breather mask to save him
from poison fumes. And it is hot, so hot
the sweat drenches him and shreds his clothes
as he bends to plunge his shovel
where the earth's bile has found its way to surface.
When he catches fire, he'll roll in a patch of moss
then simply rise and carry on. He will scoop
this *pahoehoe*, he will think of Pompeii
and the bodies torqued in final grotesque poses.
Locals cannot haul away their wooden churches fast enough,
they call this the wrath of Madame Pele,
the curse of a life that was so good
they should have known to meet it with suspicion.
But this man steps into the dawn and its yellow flames,
spins each iridescent blue clod in the air
before spreading it on a smooth rock ledge to study.
First he tries to see what this catastrophe is saying.
Then, with a trowel in his sweaty, broiling hand,
he works to sculpt it into something human.

FROM THE OCCUPIED ZONE

Even as I am easing off the pool's white tiles
I think of them, all one hundred million of those
tiny Jolly Rogers, this morning's fleet
of sperm. Even as I reach my hand
to cup that first blue stroke of water,
I see them rushing toward their target—
the egg flushed with the luster of its making
like a factory gleaming at night out on the desert.
While my heart revs its loud unsteady motor,
legs and armor crawling into the gulf,
I see myself passing through the Suez,
mother-ship with all her hands on deck,
the million faces held into the wind, the million stories
from our own conquered states—dusty jukeboxes and
pale angora sweaters, pickup trucks and girls
whose breasts are as soft as kittens.
Now these kids are waving from the deck;
they are smiling at a barren, foreign land
where some will wave their flag and some will curse them.
Their courage fills my lungs with quicker breaths:
they will whip and flap their tails
even though they know their cause is hopeless,
they are lost in a desert, they will come home in defeat.
So I flap my arms, I whip my legs.
My shadow moves along the bottom,
dark thing amplified to twice my size, and when I hit
the far wall, I drive myself into the tiles.
Suddenly, I don't want any one of them to die.
But even before that breath lets go, I think again
and flip, launching myself back to where I started.

WOMEN WHO SLEEP ON STONES

Women who sleep on stones are like
brick houses that squat alone in cornfields.
They look weatherworn, solid, dusty,
torn screens sloughing from the window frames.
But at dusk a second-story light is always burning.

Used to be I loved nothing more
than spreading my blanket on high granite ledges
that collect good water in their hollows.
Stars came close without the trees
staring and rustling like damp underthings.

But doesn't the body foil what it loves best?
Now my hips creak and their blades are tender.
I can't rest on my back for fear of exposing
my gut to night creatures who might come along
and rip it open with a beak or hoof.

And if I sleep on my belly, pinning it down,
my breasts start puling like baby pigs
trapped under their slab of torpid mother.
Dark passes as I shift from side to side
to side, the blood pooling just above the bone.

Women who sleep on stones don't sleep.
They see the stars moving, the sunrise, the gnats
rising like a hairnet lifted from a waitress's head.
The next day they're sore all over and glad
for the ache: that's how stubborn they are.

ON BELAY

Should we fall, we've got protection:
hex bolts jammed into the cracked face of this rock.
I play out rope as you climb, your shoulder-blade bones
punching at the female contours on your back.
Truth is, you're not too good yet at this sport
where nothing can be taken back or done again.
So you warn me not to tell you if
the chocks pop out, and I don't, I just watch them
shuttle down the rope to clang against what holds.
I'm thinking of your mother, Rose,
in her New Jersey kitchen making gravy:
what she would say now if she saw you here,
one finger's breadth away from falling
and bashing out your brains against these rocks.
What she wanted for you most
was protection: a lawyer husband, your hair
made a helmet the first Thursday of every month,
a son named Anthony or Francis. She rakes her fingers
against her throat, mouths one fricative oath
before she throws another pork bone in the pot.
I look up to see you hanging by one arm
and wonder what good this rope can do us now
that your mother has sworn all twelve sides of the dice
are painted black: Sylvio's bypass, the world
gone to hell in a basket and what we hold to
just a temporary ledge. But isn't that why
we've come here after all, to waver on the seam
between this life and nothing, like love's
clenched fist, like the egg that each month zippers off
the milky surface of the ovary, before
its downward spiral, its sidereal crash and burn?
And we're already goners, should we fall or not.

THINKING ABOUT ILLNESS
AFTER READING ABOUT
TENNESSEE FAINTING GOATS

Maybe they're brethren, these beasts bred clumsy,
hobbling stiff-legged over cheatgrass tufts.
Prized for how they'll freeze unpredictably
then fall, rehearsing their overwrought deaths.
Sometimes it's the woman who brings the meal
who sets them off by wearing yellow slacks,
or sometimes the drumming a certain wheel
makes on the road's washboard. Stopped in their tracks
they go down like drunks: Daisy and Willow
drop always in tandem, while Boot will lean
his fat side first against the hog-hut door.
How cruel, gripes a friend. But maybe they show
us what the body's darker fortunes mean—
we break, we rise. We do what we're here for.

I I I

I can do you blood and love without the rhetoric, and I can do you blood and rhetoric without the love, and I can do you all three concurrent or consecutive, but I can't do you love and rhetoric—they're all blood, you see.

—Tom Stoppard,
Rosencrantz and Guildernstern Are Dead

COMPULSORY TRAVEL

Not yet did we have personalities to interfere
with what we were: two sisters, two brothers.
Maybe our parents really were people who walked in the world,
were mean or kind, but you'd have to prove it to us.
They were the keepers of money, the signers of report cards,
the drivers of cars. We had a station wagon.
Back home we even had a dog, who was fed
by a neighbor kid while we toured the Jersey shore.
We waded in the motel pool and clung
to the edge of the deep end, because we couldn't swim.
Maybe that's why we never went in the ocean, despite
hours of driving. We could've just gone down the block!
Yet each year we made a ritual of this week
spent yelling and cursing and swatting each other,
with none of the analyses we now employ, the past
used as ammunition, the glosses from our latest therapist.
Back then a sock in the jaw could set anyone straight.

On Sunday afternoon, the homeward traffic would grind still
where the turnpike bottlenecked. My father
would slam his forehead against the steering wheel,
start changing lanes and leaning on the horn.
Without breeze through the window, the car would hold
our body heat like an iron skillet, skin peeling
from our burned shoulders as we hurled pretzels
and gave the finger to kids stopped in cars beside us.
My mother wouldn't mention the turn we'd missed
a few miles back; instead she'd fold the map
and jam it resolutely in the glove box while we crept on.
Perhaps this was our finest hour, as the people

we were becoming took shape and began to emerge:
the honkers of horns and the givers of fingers.
After the sun turned red and disappeared, we rolled
through darkness, wondering if the world knew all its names:
Wickatunk, Colts Neck, Zarephath, Spotswood—in every town
there were houses, in every house a light.

THE TONE

It wasn't a bell, it was a steady tone.
We folded our papers and closed our books.
Raised the wood lids of our metal desks.
Books placed inside, pens lined neatly in the tray.
Lunches taken out, necks of the brown bags
rolled and sweaty in our fists. Mrs. Flint
blowing the whistle that hung always around her neck.
Lining, in alphabetical order according to surname,
first name in the case of there being two Smiths,
along the east wall, away from the windows.
Us reciting our names, her checking the roster.
Her opening the classroom door and us waiting
for her to step to head the line. Shuffling forward
like a many-legged worm. Peter Zeigler delegated
to close the door and shut the lights. Merging
behind homerooms 212 and 214, single file against
both sides of the hallway, using banisters
as we carefully descended the stairs. One flight
then the next, turning into a basement corridor
and a room without window or light. Each class
instructed to sit Indian-style on the floor.
To press our faces into our open, knitted hands.
To keep eyes closed. To wait.
And the mindless way we executed our submission—
not running as we fled down corridors
for our lives, not wriggling not poking
each other, not spitting or talking or committing
small crimes of recess mayhem, not rehearsing our
willful farts, not wadding our sandwiches into balls
and winging them against the cinder block, not

asking to be let upstairs to pee or what to do
when the flash came that would reveal to us
the bones in our hands through our downed eyelids
not asking what comes later not asking anything
of proof or purpose beyond the insistent tone.

RUTTER'S FIELD

My father parted the barbed wires and eased me through
    as though this were another of my births.
The moon was bright enough to show each grass blade
    rippling with his steps.
Rutter's Field was burning. And the old house, filled
    with a hundred years of
dust and newspapers and sloughed-off cells belonging
    to the dead, was being thrown
like splats of orange paint against the tall black night
    through which I rode
on my father's shoulders: funny now to think, but he was
    young, still a boy.
Men were running in all different ways, water arcing
    slowly from their buckets,
while their sooty portraits flared up in the eyes
    of swaybacked horses
who bucked and spun in circles. The house was there,
    then it was gone—
though the way its windows flexed then shattered
    just before the roofbeam dropped
reappeared each time my eyes choked shut from smoke;
    that's how I knew my head was changing.
No longer was its dome full of empty space
    through which things slipped like threadless needles
then were gone. From here on,
    things would stick.
The world had stepped inside me like a man whose boots
    ring loudly on the floor—
this was memory. And soon I'd learn about his retinue:
    shame and longing and regret.

But that night on my father's shoulders all I saw was
        the flames' orange teeth and
colorless cores, the infinite shapes and voices spawning,
        the fields just waiting to be burned.

LIMITS

The dead man.
Every now and again, I see him.
And the wildlife refuge where I worked then,
the shallow ponds of Leslie Salt Company
patchworking the San Francisco Bay edges
and spreading below the hills like broken tiles,
each pond a different color—from blue to green
to yellow until finally the burnished red
of terra-cotta, as the water grew denser
and denser with salt. Dunlins blew upwards
like paper scraps torn from a single sheet,
clouds of birds purling in sunlight, harboring
the secret of escaped collision. And
that other miracle: how these weightless tufts
could find half their way to Tierra del Fuego
and make it back before spring's first good day.
On those good days, a group from the charity ward
named after the state's last concession to saints
would trudge up the hill to the visitor center,
where I'd show them California shorebirds
—a stuffed egret, western sandpiper, and avocet
whose feathers were matted and worn to shafts
from years of being stroked like puppies.
As I guided their hands over the pelts
questions stood on my tongue—mostly
about what led them to this peculiar life,
its days parceled into field trips
and visits to the library for picture books
with nurses whose enthusiasms were always greater
than their own. Their own stalled out
before reaching the moist surface of their eyes,

some of the patients fitting pigeonholes built
in my head, like *Down's syndrome* and *hydrocephaly.*
But others were not marked in any way,
and their illnesses cut closer to the bones
under my burnt-sienna ranger uniform.
Maybe I was foolish to believe in escape
from the future carried in their uncreased palms:
our lives overseen by the strict, big-breasted nurse
who is our health or our debts or even
our children, the *her* who is always putting crayons
and lumps of clay in our hands, insisting
we make our lives into some crude but useful thing.
And one day a man, a patient who must have been
supervised by his strict heart, fell down
suddenly and hard, on his way up the hill.
Two nurses prodded him on toward the building,
where he went down again like a duffel bag full of earth
in front of the reception desk where I was sitting.
I watched the one male nurse turn pale as ash
when he knelt to certify the heartbeat
of this man whose lips were blue and wet.
The other nurse took the group to the auditorium,
saying *James isn't feeling very well right now.*
James is sick. Get away from him. Then I heard
the dopey music of the automated slide show
behind those doors from which she never reappeared.
The male nurse was too young to leave stranded
with a man down on the smooth wood floor:
his cheeks still velvet, his dark fingers
worrying the valleys of the man's white wrist.
He's okay, He's breathing, as the man's skin

turned the same gray slapped on the hulls of ships,
his mouth open, a cherry sore at either edge.
I don't remember what I did at first,
I must have puttered off to perform some
stupid task that would seem useful—
gathering premoistened towelettes
or picking up the phone while the nurse repeated
He's okay, He's breathing. But the colors
got worse until nothing could spare me
from having to walk my hand in the crease
of the man's blue throat, where his carotid
should have pulsed. Nothing.
I said *You breathe for him and I'll compress*,
and for a while we worked together like a clumsy
railroad handcar, me humping at arm's length
over the ribs, the nurse sealing his lips around
the man's scabbed mouth, while yellow mucus
drained from James's eyes and nose and throat.
Each time the nurse pressed his mouth to the man's
like a reluctant lover, the stink of cud
was on his lips when he lifted up. Sometimes
he had to hold his face out to the side,
to catch a few breaths of good salt air.
Until he was no longer able to choke back his gut
and asked if I would trade places with him.
For a minute I studied the man's stoved-in chest,
which even my small knuckles had banged to jelly,
then the yellow pulp that flecked the nurse's lips,
that sour, raw smell from their mix of spit.
And I said: *No. I don't think I could . . .*

* *

It's strange what we do with the dead
—burning them or burying them in earth—
when the body always tries to revert to water.
Later, a doctor called to say the man's heart
had exploded like a paper sack: death hooked him
before he even hit the floor. So everything we did
was useless—we might as well have banged a drum
and blown into a horn. And notice how I just said "we"—
as though the nurse and I had somehow married
spirits in a pact of gambled blood, when in truth
the nurse, like the man, rode off in an ambulance,
the man for a pointless go-round in the ER, the nurse
for a shot of gamma-globulin, while I stood
in the parking lot, picking lint off my shirt.
End of story. Except that since then James
has followed me, sometimes showing up at the house
to read my gas meter, sometimes behind the counter
where he asks what I owe. No surprise then
that I've made my life with another James,
who swears my biggest defect is still the limits
on what I'll bring myself to do for someone else.
I know there are people who'll cut out their kidney
to replace a friend's cankered one, people
who'll rush into burning buildings to save the lives
of strangers. But every time I ponder selflessness
I hear the beats of my heart, that common loon,
most primitive of birds. Then life seems most
like a naked, frail thing that must be protected,
and I have suddenly become its mother, paddling
furiously with my own life saddled on my back.
There's one last thing I didn't mention—

when I refused to breathe for the dying James
what happened next was that I began to laugh:
a thin laugh, nervous laugh . . . but loud enough
to drift outside, where it stood on the hill
and creaked its wings a minute before lifting—
over the levees, across those shallowest of waters.

JULY 4, 1966

Glowing punks were clamped between our teeth
as we waited for the dark to turn
our itchy summer skin a cooler blue.
Waited for the fireworks to shoot
from the bridge that lifted its shoulders
where the river ran wide. There a lucky man
would be sticking butts of rockets
in a pail of sand: the Shooting Lotus,
Fox and Hen, the Fire Buddha with Report . . .
In the night beyond our dimming vision,
he would touch his punk to the fuse
like God waking Adam in the Sistine Chapel,
only backward, because he was a man
and the rocket was god. Five days ago
American boys in Skyhawk bombers
had raked the night above Haiphong.
And as we strained the opaque silence
for the whine of bombs and engines overhead,
we could have sworn we felt them coming,
the thrill of gory havoc in our bones.
When the starbursts finally appeared,
we saw cities burning all across the sky;
for half an hour, the rockets flared
and ricocheted so loud our jaws ached.
When it was over, my brother set down
a smuggled Bombing Plane on top a rock,
lit it, and threatened to push one of us
into the conflagration. But instead of roaring
upward with a trail of sparks and gases,
the rocket coughed and wallowed in the sedge.
Far away, on terraces of grand, colonial hotels

boys not much older than ourselves
were drinking beer, recounting victories
while the limbless wounded jeered and crawled
like crabs across the tile. The soldiers
must have kept their eyes fixed on their own
white faces, the way we locked our sights
onto the pale moon of my brother's face—
looking duped & swindled, in the end afraid
to see what lay there hissing on the ground.

OLD STORY

The first Chinese brother has drowned a boy,
for that he'll be killed. *See,* the judge says,
what burdens fall on those who can swallow the sea,
and slates him for tomorrow's guillotine.
Luckily, he has a brother with an iron neck
and one who won't burn; one can't be smothered,
and the fifth one's head just bobs like a melon
when he's tossed in the sea (his legs stretch deep.)
Death gets passed from one brother to the next
like a bowl of rice from which they all eat.
Each day, the villagers, gathered
in their black felt shoes, in their disappointment
march home, where they hit their dogs with sticks.

It is only fair, the judge says, five times,
when each brother asks to go and kiss his mother
once again good-bye. All night the five of them lie
with their heads together, legs out
like spokes of the wheel that rolls them
round this old story, the story where we all
possess someone who wants to swap us for our death—
Old Yeller or Jesus or even Mary Ann, the steam shovel
who, for our human sake, digs a hole so deep
it becomes her grave. As I lie curled in the sickle
of my mother's arm, she flips the pages,
pointing to each repetition of his face, his mouth
always drawn in a smug, pencil-thin smile, even
as those other mouths—the chopping block, the stake—
draw inversely larger, showing him their teeth.
She takes pains to show me

how no one really dies in the end, which is forgiveness.
That old story, which makes us crazy enough
to lift our hair and let our brother's blade descend.

NEEDLES

So first there's the chemo: three sticks, once a week,
    twenty-six weeks.
Then you add interferon: one stick, three times a week,
    forever.
And then there's the blood tests. How many blood tests?
    (Too many to count.)
Add all the sticks up and they come down to this: either
    your coming out clean
or else . . . well, nobody's talking
    about the *B* side,
an *or else* that plows through your life like a combine
    driven at stock-car speed,
shucking the past into two piles: *things that mattered*
    and *things that didn't.*
And the first pile looks so small when you think of
    everything you haven't done—
never seeing the Serengeti or Graceland, never running
    with the bulls in Spain.
Not to mention all the women you haven't done yet!—
    and double that number of breasts.
Okay—
    you've got a woman, a good woman make no mistake.
But how come you get just one woman when you're getting
    many lifetimes' worth of sticks?
Where was the justice in that? You feel like someone
    who's run out of clean clothes
with laundry day still half a week away; all those women
    you tossed in the pile
marked *things that didn't matter,* now you can't help but
    drag them out.
Like the blonde on trail crew who lugged the chain saw

on her shoulder up a mountain
and bucked up chunks of blighted trees, how could you
    have forgotten
how her arms quaked when the saw whined and the muscles
    went liquid in her quads,
or the sweaty patch on her chest where a mosaic formed
    of shiny flies and moss?
Or that swarthy-haired dancer, her underpants hooked
    across her face like the Lone Ranger,
the one your friends paid to come to the table, where
    she pawed and made you blush:
How come yer getting married when you could be muff-diving
    every night?
At college they swore it was John Dewey, they swore
    by the quadruped Rousseau,
and it took cancer to step up and punch your gut
    before you figured
that all along immortal truth's one best embodiment
    was just
some sixteen-year-old tabledancing on a forged ID
    at Ponders Corners.
You should have bought a red sports car, skimmed it under
    pale descending arms at the railroad crossing,
the blonde and brunette beside you under its moonroof
    & everything smelling of leather—
yes yes—this has been your flaw: how you have always
    turned away from the moment
your life was about to be stripped so the bone of it
    lay bare and glittering.
You even tried wearing a White Sox cap to bed, but its bill
    nearly put your wife's eye out.

So now you're left no choice but going capless, scarred;
        you must stand erect;
you must unveil yourself as a bald man in that most
        treacherous darkness.
You remember the first night your parents left town, left
        you home without a sitter.
Two friends came over and one of them drove the Mercury
        your dad had parked stalwartly
in the drive (you didn't know how yet)—took it down
        to some skinny junkie's place
in Wicker Park, cousin of a friend of a cousin, friend
        of a cousin of a friend,
what did it matter but that his name was Sczabo.
        Sczabo!—
as though this guy were a skin disease, or a magician
        about to make doves appear.
What he did was tie off your friends with a surgical tube,
        piece of lurid chitterling
smudged with grease along its length. Then needle, spoon—
        he did the whole bit,
it was just like in the movies, only your turn turned you
        chicken (or were you defiant?—)
Somebody's got to drive home, and that's what you did
        though you'd never
made it even as far as the driveway's end before your dad
        put his foot over the transmission hump
to forestall some calamity he thought would compromise
        the hedges.
All the way back to Evanston you piloted the Mercury
        like General Montgomery in his tank,
your friends huddled in the back seat, spines coiled,

arms cradled to their ribs—
as though each held a baby being rocked too furiously
    for any payoff less than panic.
It's the same motion your wife blames on some blown-out
    muscle in her chest
when at the end of making love she pitches violently,
    except instead of saying
something normal like *god* or *jesus* she screams *ow! ow!*
    and afterwards,
when you try sorting out her pleasure from her pain,
    she refuses you the difference.
Maybe you wish you took the needle at Sczabo's place—
    what's one more stick
among the many you'll endure, your two friends not such
    a far cry from being women,
machines shaking and arching in the wide back seat
    as Sczabo's doves appeared—
or so you thought then, though now you understand
    all the gestures the body will employ
just to keep from puking. Snow was damping the concrete
    and icing the trees,
a silence stoppered in the back of your friends' throats
    as you let the Mercury wheel pass
hand over hand, steering into the fishtails, remembering
    your dad's admonition:
when everything goes to hell the worst you can do
    is hit the brakes.

AUTUMN, 1939

In his dacha at Sochi, the great hall windows
look out on two pines. Beyond them, the sea.
Stalin is dancing, staggering, stamping . . .
His wineglass drains and fills
like the shoreline.
The trees are stiff
and straight, a pair of soldiers.
He calls the first one *restraint*
and the second *abandon.* Stalin is dancing.
His fused left toes (the second and third)
in their black boot pound the imported tile,
while his left arm, the stunted one, whirls
and slaps his thigh. Katyn,
Lvov, Vinnitsa . . . their dead heaped
and congealed in solid blocks, the pedestals
on top of which he is stomping. His lungs
bellowing like a loud machine.
That morning, the sun was a thief,
and abandon stood in the long shadows of restraint.
But now, late afternoon, when the sun
drops and tilts the shadows backward on their heels . . .
Stalin is dancing, and likewise
the pine trees are staggering in the wind.
Beyond them, the sea called black has swallowed everything.

THE DOUBLE ISSUE

August, no rain in weeks, the radio
blabbing all day from the porch
about cold war's collapse.
So now there is only Here and Us.
Meanwhile the grass has deadened
past any hope for its reprieve.
Only weeds reign, a chaos taller
than the dog's red tail: stalks
of dandelion and pigweed pretty enough
to convince me I could do without the rest,
the bluegrass and rose's constant demand
for care. Then the screwdriver
I've been using to gouge out roots
gets shoved mumblety-peg-wise into the dirt
and I go inside to lie on the sofa,
thumb through a library copy
of the world's report: commemorating
fifty years since Roosevelt shipped
blood and iron east, and stones
fell from the lintels overhanging Dresden.
Already the stout German women
are gaining on their tears, already
the small boy's stuck, forever nudged
by a gun barrel toward the waiting train,
rucksack strapped to his shoulders,
palms in the air and eyes as big
as two white bulbs dug from the earth.
Above him someone has scribbled *More
Jewish hate propaganda!* with a ballpoint
arrowing to mark the boy, and words

hung like a leather harness around his neck:
Survived! Now a multimillionaire in England!

I put down the magazine and go outside
where the blond weeds have conquered.
Goatsbeard, fleabane: their bent limbs
walking clockwise round the wind. Back
on my knees then, stabbing a Phillips head
in their buried troops—*self-heal, buttercup*—
even though the earth holds on until
it breaks. And each snapped root
gives their leagues a wilder flourishing.

THREE ZEN POEMS WITH
MY MOTHER AND CROWS

1.

My mother has started feeding the crows.
She's read that they're smart, can be named,
can learn to come when she calls.
She calculates the kind of food that crows
might like: boiled eggs and cold macaroni.

2.

Her five-gallon pot's not needed now
for dinners, with her children gone.
So on the porch she bangs its graniteware
with a chewed wood spoon, as black eyes
gauge the distance from her to safety.

3.

Under a Judas tree, my mother's noodles
at the yard's far end, where crows
crack the dry leaves after she retreats.
She has named them all Lucky or Midnight.
With time, my mother says, she'll lure them in.

MONORAIL

He stands by the helm, his face full of blue
from the buildings at twilight, his hand
knuckled around a metal pole that keeps him
from falling, as he flies past the vaults
of startled mannequins, the red ohs their lips.
Christmas lights are also falling
through the windshield, onto his chest:
right side green, left side red—
dark then back again.

Wait . . . my father is not moving yet:
no one has claimed the worn-leather throne.
But his thoughts are moving, wondering
if movement is the same as growing old
in the province of space, not time. Inside his shoes,
his toes are as blue as the city streets,
and the drum in his chest, his red-lit chest,
is growing dim. He knows the train he's about to ride
has one rail: no steering, no turns.
And the only skill is in the brake.

The brake. His lips roll over the words:
The Dead-Man's Brake. And a small boy
—come to ride up front—hears him,
tugs my father's coat and asks:
Hey mister, are you the driver of this train?

I V

The other day it was so good.
There was already a little bit of eternity
in my intestines.

—Rainer Maria Rilke

"WHAT ONE LOVES ARE
THINGS THAT FADE"

No matter how sweetly it begins, not long
into lovemaking I will see their faces—
there but not there, like creatures inseparable
from the dusk that stirs them to the clearing.
This time, it's the nuns who were forced
off the road near Santa Ana: camp shirts
disheveled round their necks, their fingers
tangled with the amber rosaries and
concussive gunfire of the tropics.
Ghosts that come stippled by the TV news
beamed down so relentlessly from space.
Ghosts of the Wirephoto, ghosts of the biopic,
ghosts that sometimes arrive incarnate
like the risen dead. Like the woman I dined with
who parted her hair during the coffee and sweets
to show me the trench knocked into her skull
with a brick. She couldn't remember a thing,
not what he looked like or how his hands felt
on her skin. But surely what was struck
from the broken slate of her included this:
quick breaths in the face and the body spinning
down its own dark shaft. How loud the queue
of women gathered at the doorjamb, clamoring
to braid themselves into that falling.
And after they go, worse, the spotlit quiet—
when comes the cry that I swear isn't mine.

FOR MY WASHER AND DRYER

I like the dental white of them, like a beauty contestant's
    square capped teeth;
I forgive their clanging, the way they hump across the floor
    with unbalanced loads.
But most of all I'm grateful for their having saved me
    from hours spent otherwise
washed in light from the laundromat's fluorescent fixture,
    that cemetery of a thousand flies.
An old black-and-white would be buzzing in the corner
    for an audience of molded plastic chairs
where last year's magazines and a few men have been spacing
    out a talk show's drone,
the picture slipping northward band by band, until someone
    summons the courage to slam
a fist (*bam!*) on the console, restoring the vertical hold, .
    at the same time routing us
from the stupors we wear like a cowboy's chaps, so as not
    to get stuck
in the brambles of an errant hard-luck story
    beside the change machine.

This would be the moment she enters, into this crushed lull
    of a resurrected Geraldo:
young woman wrestling six black garbage bags through
    the laundromat door.
Two children stripped to their underwear trail behind her
    like caged birds chirping.
For almost an hour she hauls the dirty sheets and pj's
    from washer to dryer,
the fabric worn thin as the frail threads of her patience,
    barking, *Get over here.*

Finally her ride shows up, a short guy whose jeans
    straddle his ass low.
But the last quarter on her dryer hasn't cycled through,
    and he's got to kill time staggering
the aisles, suffering the accusation of women's underthings
    and soiled oven mitts,
the sputum and rheum that his own kids cough up
    from God knows what recess.
Until this laundry overcomes him: he yanks the magazine
    out of her hands so she'll have to

Look at him, goddamnit! before he ups and hauls the boy
    outside, to their dented sedan.
When she runs after, he makes a fleshy chrysanthemum
    with his right fist
and slams it into her face, dumping her backward while
    he peels out,
leaving her saddle-legged, stunned, with the baby girl
    crawling circles on the curb.
The rest of us stare out the window, and I imagine what
    she sees from outside looking in:
our mouths are open, our faces green in this light,
    we are crueler than he is,
our good intentions have always drawn interest
    on someone else's hard luck.
She raises a hand to shield her face, her head wagging
    sideways as if to signal
that our most welcome kindness would be turning away now,
    resuming the stupor:
folding clothes in our baskets and hurrying them home
    while the wicker is warm.

The next day I calculated my retreat: the Sears revolving
    charge card, the finance plan.
And in this way I let him win, making his fist the fat root
    of my own gain.
How many of our comforts rose from the cruelties of men—
    De' Medici's tomb,
the Nazi Volkswagen, the origin of lipstick
    in a bloodied mouth?
Sometimes these relics of the man-made world make me ashamed
    about the circuits of my desires.
Like the day those two guys in greasy coveralls showed up
    and lifted the appliances
over their heads, high over the fence because the boxes
    wouldn't fit through the gate.
When they entered my yard, I understood how the women felt
    when Allied troops rolled into France:
I wanted to pelt them with roses, bring them baskets full
    of linens and exotic fruits.
I was ready to get on my knees, kiss the scuffed leather
    of their steel-toed, Red Wing boots.

THE MARSHALL STREET POSTER
OF MARILYN MONROE

I go by you every day, White Lady, I go by.
In the window of the Pakistani's head shop, you stand
over the hookahs and toe rings, Zigzag and EZ Wider.
Bent toward me in your black-net jet-bead
skin-tight nothing, your breasts don't spare me anything
except the nipples. Those you keep for yourself,
the ruby quarters you'll let drop in no one's slot,
while your hands hang palm-outward like a begged
question, gimmee-gimmee-gimmying around your knees.

Me, I sweep the butcher shop next door,
where the meat is skinned and flayed and swings
on hooks, slowly in the window. The blood
gets washed down drains, but the smell lingers.
For lunch, a dozen chicken wings from Sal's Birdland,
and I sit on the broken wall at front-row center,
watching you across the street, how you eye the cars
laying their cataracts of soot. My teeth
gnaw at hollow bones while I think of angels.

Like these dumb clucks, our lives are spent
in cages that have made our bodies thick, useless
for sex or flight. Instead they hook us up
and suck us dry: I could run my lips
across your glass pane and still leave no trace.
White Lady, Little Sheba, Madonna of the Snows—
your hair is the color of blank paper or heroin
or a clean set of sheets, the nostrils
and lashes black as Chinese words. At seventeen

you learned to smile with your lips half-open,
your tongue paused in the hollow of your mouth—
and I can't keep my eyes off it, like my own tongue
working on a broken tooth. Each day this street
goes black then white then black again and nothing
seems to change. Oh my white pearl,
my platinum timepiece, my no-rust Amazon—
your being dead now might just be a good thing
'cause if you weren't dead, you'd probably just be old.

ARCHAEOLOGY OF THE BED

At ten, I knew all the geologic periods: Cambrian,
Ordovician, Silurian. Each stratum yielding its indigenous
beasts, the trilobites and cephalopods and chitons.
But for real treasures you had to dig deep.
In my parents' bedroom, I went down through the layers:
spread, blanket, blanket, top sheet, bottom sheet,
mattress. There, on top of the boxsprings'
chintz: *Argosy, Evergreen, Playboy,* magazines
bearing portents of my body's *que sera:* breasts
that would mushroom over some damp night, the sleek
curve of the waist, the tender moist sump of the armpit.
That was all you got back then, maybe a silhouetted
buttock where it swelled then slipped into the thigh.

When daring, I would kidnap her for burial
in the ruined stockroom of Mr. Phillips's class,
in his stacks of *Children's Highlife,* whose sketches
were an insult, fossils of a life we were leaving
behind. Instead we skimmed the ads for liquor
and Van Heusen shirts, a man whose conquests glinted
from his tie tack, from the onyx link at his cuff.
But even his gem-studded cartilage couldn't
stay our pages turning, his body
never intricate enough to mine for bones.
Paging on, we struck our shovels right into destiny,
little women sounding the navels of bigger women
who would, like coelacanths, uncloak their secret lungs.
And we wanted a signal, wanted to see them rise
from their primeval soup, water-beaded and glittering,
glittering like the first fish stepping onto earth.

BLACK GIRLS

Even magazines like *Tiger Beat* didn't print their pictures,
and Ed Sullivan, you could tell, felt as though
he'd just been visited by men from Mars
when they showed up in their poodle skirts and gloves,
twirling and dipping beneath conked beehives
or flips, with satin bows above the bangs, and yards
of pink taffeta so stiff it never rustled.
Our town's one black family six boys, no girls,
so mothers made sure to walk us home from school.
The Supremes, Little Eva, Martha Reeves
whooping *Heat Wave* up our dirndls, across
cracked leatherette at Broadway Luncheonette
where ruin started with an egg cream, a Lucky Strike
flinted on two quarters in the boothside juke.
Later, when the first high-school girl got pregnant
and Mother said *I just want to see the color on that child,*
I think she was missing what to be afraid of—
the Jones boys too much my own hated brothers,
with their white shirts and ties and Catholic
school slacks. Whereas these girls held secrets
in their feathery mouths, pale tongues
like birds sprung from the trapdoors of clocks.
And scrolling back again they sucked us in
to kneel there mantled inside their wet notes, screwed
to these lives spent rehearsing secret liturgies
in mirrors: the butt cocked, the flat palm
suspended, then swum behind the hip. Now
when my friend starts shimmying around the kitchen
mourning his sequins, swearing he'll be in the next life
a goddess with big straight teeth—it's "Respect"
that forces him to admit it, booming from the stereo
like a night heron flapping out of Aretha's throat.

ON THE FEMALE SERIAL KILLERS

There's a biker bar where we invent their being born
    into the world,
swallowing the Florida highway as though it were a strip
    of sweet black taffy.
When they pull onto the shoulder and open their hood,
    it's as simple as opening their legs.
Brake lights would flicker: easy enough to take their pick
    and take him for a spin.
One guy drives a sausage truck, one is a missionary
    with the Christ Is The Answer Crusade.
By backwater sloughs they keep his promises rolling,
    his bankrupt word, *anything.*
But they let the presidents sleep on the uncreased bills
    tucked in each leather wallet.
Instead they leave the empty foil of condom wrappers
    yawning in the mud beside each corpse—
no other traces. And late-night talk-show hosts erect
    their trails of reason:
fathers, drugs, insanity . . . as though the women can't exist
    apart from explanations why.
In artist renderings, both wear knitted caps: broad cheeks
    and permanent waves and windbreakers.
They look like women headed for a high-school football game
    to cheer their sons,
their cigarettes tilted heavenward between two carefully
    lacquered nails.
In quickie-markets where they idle in their battered car,
    there's no eye contact
with the boys who volunteer to fill them up; instead
    they sit in attitudes of prayer,
and the straw rising from each tub of orange soda
    to insert itself between their lips

gives not one bit of them away: how demurely they harbor
     each day's twilit pilgrimage,
with their arms out the window and net strung behind
     while the revival station
warbles out a verse from Matthew four-nineteen: *Follow me,
     and I will make you the fishers of men.*

BARBIE TELLS HER BIOGRAPHY

The day JFK was shot you laid me in the mud
and ground the boy-doll into me.
But even Ken could not commit the sin
of trespass, his organ palsied in a lump.
Child: you were breeding new America
from my petrochemical body, my breasts
two warheads aimed at Cuba, right buttock
bearing the mark of a toy empire.

You found my seams all shut: price
paid for deathless crotch, for afternoons
spent wheeling round the yard in the Dreamobile.
The Johnson years, you left me
locked for days in a vinyl coffin full of gowns.
My feet were arched in ready spasms
for those tiny spiked heels
you'd have me grind into a rival's commie eye.

By the time Bobby fell in Tinseltown,
you'd cropped my hair in tufts and scattered
all my haute couture to rain and mud.
I shuffled naked, like girls in crazy wards
searching magazines for their lost faces.
And when you find your parents dead—and they *will* die—
you'll find me buried in their basement
and wonder why you speckled me with ink tattoos.

Think then where your memory begins:
running home, lunchbox taking chinks out of your thigh,
to find your mother weeping in the kitchen,

her radio full of ghosts. Remember
how it was me, not her, you chose to comfort,
how I was dressed in pillbox pink and brought outside
to play Dallas's first lady against a hero's effigy.
How his perfect body rained in pieces on my skin.

AN AMPLIFIED GESTURE

After the actress O-sada kissed her lover all over,
her mouth on him for five days in the Arakawa hotel
like a remora cleaning the shark, she strangled him.
Such is the price of ecstasy.
His moldering body's odor finally skulked
down the hall and lured the cops, but his genitals
were gone, a theft which proved to be O-Sada's unravelling—
when they caught up with her in Shinagawa Station
the goods were on her person, wrapped in cotton
inside her obi, squashed flat against her heart.

In her picture, she looks capable of murder
but allure seems far-fetched: sharp teeth
jutting below her upper lip like a badger's teeth,
even her eyes slick like those of an animal
when its belly's full. But then I show the photo
to a friend, who sees the lodestar in O-sada's mouth.
And tells me about the girl she knew in teenage years
whose mouth was not brought into line by modern dentists.
Sitting in a car at the filling station, my friend
saw how the gas hop, just from talking to this girl, Corinne,
and watching her lip rub up and down across those teeth,
got an erection. "That thick around,"
my friend remembers after all these years,
making a circle so wide it calls for both her hands.

ANNUNCIATION AT A FOREIGN FILM

Friday night at the odeum and you're surrounded by ghosts
like these three girls lighting on the row ahead.
They're homing in on darkness's momentum,
snapping gum and sucking out its pith.
By turns they're also swigging from a juice jar,
jigging wrists to make the ice cubes clink,

and in that ill-tempered chiming you remember
the jar and the thermos and vodka otherwise snuck
into tangerines using someone's father's insulin syringe.
How the juice burned running down your throat.
How you pitched your voice a half-shriek bright
so that it spiraled overhead. Soon as it's dark

you can bet on them burying the Italian bombshell
with their snickers: they're not about
to let themselves be cowed by someone else's babe.
But by then you'll be unspooling reels inside your head
and carrying these girls piggyback like wings,
back to days before the theater's conversion—

ornate cornices gone multiplex and carpet run up
on the walls. Here in the balcony—now gutted
and boxed—you were the virgin broadcasting
from heaven, fallout from the coned projector light
dusting your skin while everybody pitted down below
made only quiet, bovine vespers. You saw

Sophia Loren pillaged in the subtitles and nothing
could make you flinch, except when a breast

appeared on-screen in such extravagant diameter
it made you want to stay buzzed forever, you
who imagined herself loud but never that conspicuous.
You needn't have worried: screens pretty soon

dwindled, and you found enough pinhead-scale angels
in the world conspiring to keep you small as dust.
And this you tap the shrillest girl to tell her,
your fingers on her shoulder's leather slope.
But the message comes out a hissing sound, the words
having drained for so many years through your clenched teeth.

DRESSAGE

It was too good, too good
the white horse dancing in the field.
We'd parked beside the rainy pasture
to watch a lone mare take her one unending
meal; instead we found her four legs crossing
and uncrossing—her trotting left
then right, as though the water-logged dirt
and its distant circumference of pines
were an arena full of satin lookers-on . . .

Too good the white horse, too good
the sad frogs telling stories in the valley,
too good the heron unfolding awkward
prehistoric wings, then lifting itself
against such doubt, such questionable odds.
And what about the cowbirds gathering
over the marsh at dusk in such numbers
they make the sky black, a spectacle
so close to holy that it leaves me dumb.

Somehow our gratitude never seems enough,
the breath knocked from our praises
and leaving us speechless in their wake.
And what about love, caught in its own dumb name
yet forgiving us even its naming?—returning faithful
on those nights when wind stirs the branches
into a sound so close to human breathing
we can never bear repeating it to one another:
It is too good. It is too good.

CAIRN FOR FUTURE TRAVEL

I was young for a minute, but then I got old.
Already the black cane stands by
the threshold, already my feet are flowerpots
in thick black shoes. So not long now
before I will have what follows:

a spidery hairnet to circle my scalp, a hand
calloused enough to whack your ear. And with them,
the deep wisdom of Sicilian great-aunts:
how to plumb for the melon's ripeness, how
to stand the loaves upright in my twine sack.

And you, are you ready? Have you brushed
your brown suitcoat and hat? Have you counted
your mahogany chessmen and oiled the zipper
on their leather case? Have you filled
your sack of crumbs for the pigeons?

In the park, men are waiting, raking
the bocce-court sand. And as for this second-floor
window where I shake my fist: soon you will learn
to feign deafness, fishing the silver ball
up from your loose, deep pocket.

THE BODY RISING

I'd like to do something that would be
the opposite of skydiving. Instead of falling
I would rise up and up . . . I guess I'm talking
about flying . . .

—letter from V. K.

Think about the girl in her red bikini,
how she rides the air behind the speedboat.
So what if her chest is leashed to a kite—
forget the kite. Think of county-fair daredevils
careering in rickety turrets, their motorbikes
riding the wall at centrifugal speeds. So what
if you paid a dollar admission—forget the dollar,
forget whatever you admitted. Think of all the times
you didn't have to pay to see gravity break:
the circus clown cannonballed into the sky,
and Eva Braun zeppelined into the sky,
and the astronauts, especially the astronauts
who never came down when they were turned to vapor.
How to find fault in anything that includes the body rising:
the raft spilling its paddlers, who disappear
so theatrically before they surface in the river's twisted
sheets; the WWII bomber that crashes into the mountain
and stays buried, whose airmen keep floating up
after years in the glacier, limb by perfect limb;
the pillar of smoke rising from the funeral home
run by your neighbors, the monosyllabic
Mills & Burns. For months you've been typing
in a second-story room across the street, oblivious
to what the stories mean—the fact you sit on nothing
more than air, you inhabit the air
just over the oldest bank vault in town, all day

you steep in the waft of silver dollars.
Yet it's not the floor that's important,
not the raft of flowered carpet you think holds everything
up; it's not the kite but the body, not the river
but the body, not the rocket but the body, that understands
its elements so well it can revert to them in a blink.
And maybe we serve the body most faithfully
when we abandon it, the way these dancers
allow themselves to rise up on each other's wings.
But these aren't dancers really: they don't have wings.
Just deathmetal punks, speedslammers, and moshers
whose choreography's zoned against unbruised escape.
The bass is a wooden shoe clogging
the deepest canal in your ear, and teenage boys
have started to launch themselves like supermans
soaring over the crowd of burnished heads.
You're thinking about what odds these boys risk
getting crushed. But look what happens next:
they don't get crushed. Instead they turn
weightless and waterlogged, bullied and buoyed
like ghosts who can't drown because they have no boats.
Vaults of pliant and complete surrender, rising
as each body passes through the pairs of upraised hands.

NOTES

For the story of the 1933 fire at a Tokyo department store that is re-
counted in the poem "How Western Underwear Came to Japan," I
would like to thank Edward Seidensticker's *Tokyo Rising: The City Since
the Great Earthquake.*

"Elephant" was written after Raymond Carver's last reading in
Seattle. "Flesh Tooth House" was inspired in part by the poetry of
his widow, Tess Gallagher.

"Retablo with Multiple Sclerosis and Saints" takes its factual infor-
mation about the life of Frida Kahlo from Hayden Herrera's biogra-
phy. I couldn't have completed the poem had I not also seen Kahlo's
collaborative "exquisite corpses" reprinted in Herrera's *Frida Kahlo: The
Paintings* and the ex-votos in Gloria Kay Gifford's *Mexican Folk Retablos.*

Stephen Lang is a sculptor who works with molten lava on Hawaii's
Big Island. The epigraph and much of what is described in the poem
"Kilned" comes from an article on Lang that appeared in *Omni* mag-
azine.

"Needles" appears with apologies to Walter.

For the anecdote and odd details about Joseph Stalin's anatomy re-
counted in "Autumn, 1939," I would like to acknowledge Robert
McNeal's *Stalin: Man and Ruler.*

"The Double Issue" was written in memory of Robert Buchanan, a
young man bludgeoned by neo-Nazis in a train tunnel in Olympia,
Washington in 1992.